SCHOLASTIC

News

Nonfiction Readers®

We Are Citizens

By Laine Falk

Children's Press®
An Imprint of Scholastic Inc.
New York Toronto London Auckland Sydney
Mexico City New Delhi Hong Kong
Danbury, Connecticut

These content vocabulary word builders are for grades 1–2.

Subject Consultant: Eli J. Lesser, MA, Director of Education, National Constitution Center, Philadelphia, Pennsylvania

Reading Consultant: Cecilia Minden-Cupp, PhD, Early Literacy Consultant and Author, Chapel Hill, North Carolina

Photographs ©2010: age fotostock/Comstock Images: 20 top; Alamy Images: 12, 23 bottom (amana images inc.), 5 bottom right (David Burton), 6, 13, 23 center (Corbis Super RF), 15 (JupiterImages/Thinkstock), 21 bottom left (Howard Sayer); Corbis Images/Tom Grill: 4, 22 bottom; Ellen B. Senisi: 20 bottom right; iStockphoto/Jan Rysavy: 16, 23 top; James Levin/Studio 10: 21 bottom right, 21 top; PhotoEdit: 5 bottom left (Myrleen Ferguson Cate), 1, 9 (Richard Hutchings), 8, 11, 20 bottom left (Michael Newman), 14 (David Young-Wolff); Superstock, Inc.: 2, 5 center left (Blend Images), cover (Corbis), 5 top right, 10, 22 top (Creatas Images); The Image Works/Nancy Richmond: 5 top left; VEER: back cover, 7, 17 (Corbis Photography), 19 (Kevin Dodge/Flirt Photography).

Art Direction and Production: Scholastic Classroom Magazines

Library of Congress Cataloging-in-Publication Data

Falk, Laine, 1974-
We are citizens / Laine Falk.
    p. cm. – (Scholastic news nonfiction readers)
Includes bibliographical references and index.
ISBN 13: 978-0-531-21349-0 (lib. bdg.) 978-0-531-21448-0 (pbk.)
ISBN 10: 0-531-21349-8 (lib. bdg.) 0-531-21448-6 (pbk.)
1. Citizenship–Juvenile literature. I. Title. II. series.
JF801.F35 2009   323.6–dc22   2009007323

CONTENTS

What Is a Citizen?

A citizen is part of a group.

You are a citizen at home.
You are a citizen at school.
You are a citizen in your **community**.

community

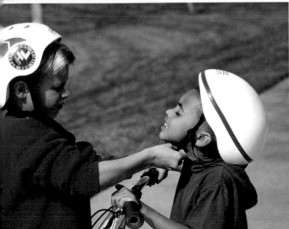

5

What Citizens Do

Citizens help out.

There are many ways you can help. This boy helps his dad rake leaves.

How do you help out in your **family**?

family

When Dad has help, raking leaves is less work.

Citizens work together.

These children clean up the **classroom** after some messy painting.

Do you sometimes work with others to get a big job done?

classroom

A friend makes the work go faster.

Citizens speak up.

This child raises his hand. Then, he shares an idea with his **classmates**.

Do you let others know when you have something to say?

classmates

This boy has a great idea to share!

11

Citizens listen.

These **teammates** take turns talking. They listen carefully to each other.

Do you listen to what other people have to say?

teammates

These teammates are making plans to win their game!

Citizens care for others.

One way to care for others is to collect cans for a **food drive**.

How can you show you care for people?

food drive

FOOD DRIVE

These cans of food will go to people who do not have enough to eat.

Citizens care for the **Earth**.

These girls pick up litter in a pond. They want the pond to be clean for everyone.

What can you do to help take care of the Earth?

Earth

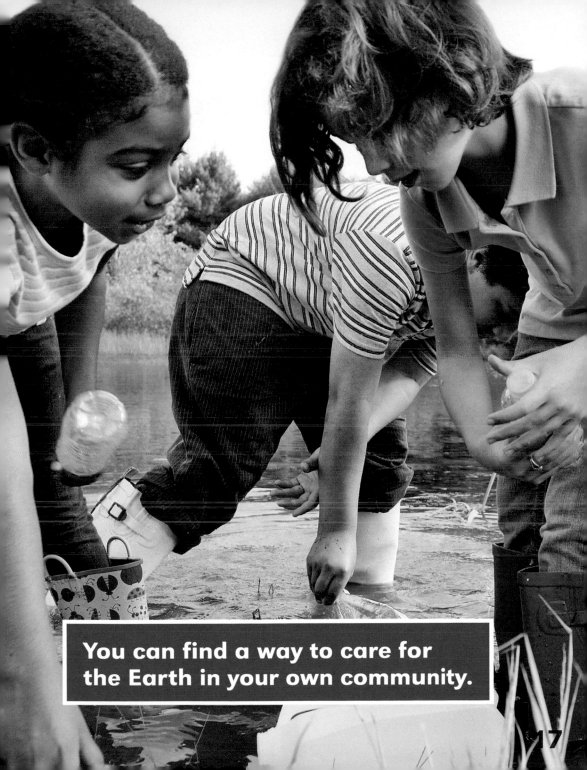

You can find a way to care for the Earth in your own community.

Citizens Belong

We are all citizens!

We belong to families. We belong to schools. We belong to communities.

We work together. We help one another. We care for one another and for our world.

BE A GOOD CLASSROOM CITIZEN!

Here is a checklist of ways to be a good citizen at school. There are other ways, too. Can you think of some of them?

✓ **Raise your hand.**

✓ **Help keep your classroom clean.**

✓ **Take good care of books.**

✓ **Listen to your teacher.**

✓ **Be kind to your classmates.**

✓ **Solve problems with words.**

YOUR NEW WORDS

classmates (**klass**-mates) people who are in the same class

classroom (**klass**-room) a room in school where classes are held

community (kuh-**myoo**-nuh-tee) a group of people who live near each other or who have something in common

arth (urth) the planet where we live

mily (**fam**-uh-lee) a group of people who are related to each other

od drive (food drive) a project to collect food and give it to people who do not have enough to eat

ammates (**teem**-mates) people who are on a team together

INDEX

FIND OUT MORE

Book:

Goldish, Meish. *The Garden on Green Street*. New York: Scholastic, 2002.

Website:

PBS Kids
http://pbskids.org/zoom/activities/action/ways.html

MEET THE AUTHOR

Laine Falk is a writer and Scholastic editor. She lives in Brooklyn, New York, with her family.